This Room is Waiting

Poems from Iraq and the United Kingdom

FREIGHT BOOKS

First published in the UK April 2014
By Freight Books
49-53 Virginia Street
Glasgow, G1 1TS
www.freightbooks.co.uk

A CIP catalogue reference for this book is available from the British Library.

ISBN 978-1-908754-49-3

Typeset by Freight in Adobe Caslon Pro and Adobe Arabic
Printed and bound by Bell and Bain, Glasgow

the publisher acknowledges investment from
Creative Scotland toward the publication of this book

Reel Arts
www.reelfestivals.org

Making Literature Travel

Contents

Introduction

'What's the Arabic for aphrodisiac?' someone shouted into the conference room of Kurdistan's 'Swedish Village', home to the eight poets of Reel Iraq 2013. Cue a twenty minute debate on what gets people going in the Middle East and whether broccoli is as exciting as oysters.

This is how we work. In January 2013 Reel Festivals brought four British poets (John Glenday, Jen Hadfield, William Letford and Krystelle Bamford) to the Kurdish mountain village of Shaqlawa to meet with four Iraqi poets (Zaher Mousa, Ghareeb Iskander, Awezan Nouri Hakeem and Sabreen Kadhim). Working with the 'bridge' translations I had prepared in advance, the poets sat in pairs - with an interpreter on hand - and chatted about each others' work. Can you swear in Arabic poetry? Should you translate a Scots word into Modern Standard Arabic or a dialect and if so, which one? Which register of speech is more engaging, more poetic? And that golden question which everyone always wants to ask but doesn't really dare: what do you actually mean by that?

As each poet spoke little or none of the other's language, and as they all brought their own style and sensibilities to the verse, we consider these literary outcomes as 'versions' rather than pure translations. The new works produced - in Arabic, Kurdish and English - not only share the essence of the original poem, but also convey new cultural resonances in the corresponding language. They became acts of friendship and solidarity; the translation of each poet's reality. Yet despite the obvious differences in context, the works themselves demonstrate how poetry can transcend national boundaries and languages. These poems tell us stories of war, but also of lousy boyfriends and the elusiveness of time.

Reel Festivals collaborates with artists working in areas of conflict to celebrate diversity, build solidarity and create dialogue with audiences internationally. Through live events and festivals, we explore alternative stories and aim to challenge stereotypes. March 2013 marked the ten year anniversary of the invasion of Iraq. Media representation too often offers only a negative and damaging portrayal of the country and as a response we wanted to celebrate the resilience of the people and the diversity of culture throughout this protracted conflict. Places of culture are often among the first victims of tyranny and war. For so long a place synonymous with literary invention, the last few decades have seen Baghdad become a place of censorship and fear. But Iraqis both inside and outside the country continue to create, to engage and to play. Iraq is not just the one-time 'cradle of civilisation', Iraqi culture is alive today and we wanted to share it.

These poems were first presented at the British Council's Erbil Literature Festival, and we are hugely grateful to them for helping make these workshops possible. Reel Festivals then toured with the eight poets around the UK in March 2013 as part of our Reel Iraq festival. Our heartfelt thanks also go to Dina Mousawi and Hoshang Waziri for contributing their Arabic and Kurdish interpretation, with both insight and wit. And none of this would have been possible without the vision and dynamism of Dan Gorman (Reel Iraq Project Director) and Ryan Van Winkle (Reel Iraq Literature Director).

Within these pages you will also find four newly commissioned pieces of Kufic Calligraphy incorporating phrases from some of the poems, drawn by Samir Sumaida'ie. They stand not only as beautiful works of art in themselves, but also as testament to the link between the visual and the literary in both Iraq and the UK.

'This Room is Waiting' brings you some of the most exciting voices in Iraq and the United Kingdom, but it is also an ode to the power of literature and friendship in crossing boundaries and bearing witness. Iraq and its people may still be waiting for peace and justice, but meanwhile its people continue to play, innovate, and explore realities of their own through poetry and the arts. We owe much to Iraq's contribution to our own 'civilisation' and, I believe, we still have much to learn.

Lauren Pyott
Reel Iraq Literature Coordinator and Arabic Translator

It's Writing on my Hand

أن تكتب علي يدي

From 'Water my Heart with a Jonquil'
(Sabreen Kadhim / Krystelle Bamford)
Kufic Calligraphy by Samir Sumaida'ie

لەگەڵ تێپەربوونی کات گەیشتین بە یەک .. یەکمان بینی

ولیام لیتفۆرد

تیشکی مۆمەکە بەنەرمی دەنیشتە سەر روخساری

گەرچی چەتاڵەکەی دەستی هێندە سەنگین نیه

وەلێ بە ئەستەم بەرزی دەکاتەوە

پێدەچێ ئەسپارەگۆسی چەشتبێ

دووانەکان وەکو شەبەنگ بەدەوریدا ئاڵابوون

دواتر چەشنی وردە شەپۆل لێ دوور دەکەوتنەوە

پاش هەندێک لە شەراب و مەستی

جورئەتم کردو وتم:

تۆ دەبێ بە گەنجی زۆر جوان بوبی..

بێدەنگی... کەس نەمانبیستێ

مەچەکی گرتم و چپاندیە گوێم

ئێمە بەرێکەوت پێمان هەڵدەکەوێتە گەنجێتیەوە

لە شوێنێکی دیکەوە...

بەشەکەی دیکەی ژیانمان بەڕێ دەکەین بە دروستکردنی ڕێگای گەرانەوە بۆ ماڵەوە .. عەدەم

ئاوێزان نوری حکیم

وقتما اجتمعنا

ويليام لتفورد

لم يكنْ غير ضوءٍ شمعةٍ
السطوعُ الذي احتضنَ وجهها
لم تكنْ سوى إحدى أصابعها
تلكَ الشوكةُ منعدمةُ الوزن
و التي لِماماً ما ارتفعتْ
ربما كان للفُلفلِ
خطوةٌ في جسدها نحو السرير ، ربما
و مثل طوافٍ يتلاشى على الماء
كانت الأصواتُ تدورُ حول عزلتها
جزراً لا يعود

و إثر ثمالةٍ من نبيذٍ و خدر
حدثتها من قلبٍ قوي:
حقاً ، كان شبابك ورقة رابحة
وقتئذٍ رسمت مداراتها على يدي
و خفيضاً صوتها جاءني:
بقامةٍ سكرى نعثر بالنضرة
خارج الخارطة ، و نؤوب بما نزر من عمرٍ إلى لوحةٍ
في كُرّاسِ طفلٍ حالم.

زاهر موسى

2

By the Time We Met

William Letford

Candlelight was kind to her. Her fork seemed
weightless, but seldom made the journey upwards
I suspect that she had tasted asparagus before
Conversations clashed around her and dispersed
like circles on the surface of a lake
After the Shiraz, I had courage, and I said. *You
must have been something when you were younger*
Quiet, so none could overhear, she touched
my arm and replied. 'We stumble into youth
by accident, from somewhere else, and spend
the rest of our lives making our way home.'

و أنتَ

زاهر موسى

السؤالُ الذي يتبخرُ في الفم
يتكثّفُ في العيون
و أنتَ ...
سمكةٌ تُطالبُ الطُهاة بالطُعم
حصانٌ يُرخي لجامَهُ للفارس القتيل
غرابٌ يدفنُ أخاهُ ليعضَّ الآخرون أصابعهم
فأنظرْ
لك نوافذُ في رأسِكَ .. لا يُطلُّ منها غيرُ اليأس
يدٌ تمرُرها ... فيتفصدُ السطرُ كالعرق
و يُسقطُ البيانو أغُنيتَهُ جنيناً ميتاً
خطواتٌ تُلصقُها على بريدِ الشوارعِ التي لا تعود
و حذاؤك لغمٌ في الظهيرة
الأسابيعُ عملٌ تُتقنُ إنهاءَهُ
و على شاشةٍ مضاءةٍ تتدحرجُ عيونُكَ كالكرات
فاستمعْ ...
الطبلُ نبضٌ من دونِ قلب
الخطبةُ (في النهاية) مايكروفون
فلماذا حينَ تسدُّ أذنيكَ تغضبُ الأصوات؟
حينَ تغلقُ البابَ يستخدمُ الآخرونَ " أكفُهم"؟
تنامُ ... فتصرخُ الكوابيس ؟ و يحدثُكَ ميتٌ عن رغبتهِ في لقائك؟
السؤالُ الذي ينزلقُ بين أصابعك في الناي
تلدغهُ الأفعى
و أنتَ ...
قاربٌ يدعو الماء إلى ضيافته
حجرٌ يبتعدُ عن طريقِ أرجلٍ تركلُه

4

And You?

Zaher Mousa

The question which evaporates on the tongue
springs up in the eyes
and you…
are a fish begging more salt from the chef,
a warhorse lowering its reins to its rider, now dead,
a crow slaying its brother for show,
so look…
You have these windows in your mind
which only admit despair.
A hand passes over the page
and the lines are slicked with sweat
and the piano labours on, passing a stillbirth song,
and footsteps affix to the pavement like stamps on unanswered mail,
and your shoes are a landmine at noon.
The weeks turn again and again like an endless task,
and your eyes roll down the bright screen, without end,
so listen…
The drum is a heartless pulse.
The speech, only a microphone.
So why then, when you cover your ears, is it all still sound and fury?
When you bar your door the crowds surge against it?
You sleep…and the nightmares still rage? And the dead man winks and vows
to see you soon?
The question slips under your fingers like breath through a flute.
The snake lunges from his basket.
And you…

سلّمٌ يكررُ نفسهُ كي يصلَ من يصل
و محارةٌ تبالغُ في كتمانِ اللؤلؤة.

are a dinghy inviting in the sea like a friend,
a boulder afraid of the soft, kicking foot,
a ladder ascending over and over to no place, for no one,
a blind oyster, his brilliant, worthless pearl.

Krystelle Bamford

خاڵیيم له خۆم و پڕم له زیکری تۆ

ئاوێزان نوري حکیم

یارۆ گیان

له ژوورێکدام پڕه له خۆم و له تۆ نا

پڕه له قیژەی خەیاڵەکانم و دەنگی تۆ نا

پڕه له گریانەکانم و له پێکەنینی تۆ نا

پڕه له کوفرەکانم لەزیکری خودا نا

پڕه له تاریکی و له سەڵاوی خۆر نا

پڕه له چاوەڕوانی و هاتنی تۆ نا

(با) دێت له دەرگام دەدات و تۆ نا

تەنیایی شەوان له باخەڵمدا دەنوێ و تۆ نا

مەراق رومەتەکانم ماچ دەکات لێوی تۆ نا

ژوورێک

دیوارەکانی تابلۆی بەدبەختیان بەخۆدا هەڵواسیوەو

وێنەی تۆ نا

بەر پەنجەرەرم به ئینجانەی حوزن رازراوەتەوەو

نازنازی سۆزی تۆ نا

ئاخر یارۆ دەی من چی بکەم

که خاڵیيم له خۆم و له زیکری تۆ نا

وجودم چی مانایەک دەبەخشێ ئەزیزم

هەموو شتێکم کۆتایی هات

بەڵام فیراقی تۆ نا

No Room My Love

Awezan Nouri Hakeem

This room is full of me, but you, no
This room screams with thought, but your voice, no
This room is sodden with tears, but your laughter, no
This room is filled with night, but the sun, no
This room is waiting
Wind will knock the door, but you, no
Loneliness fills my embrace, but you, no
Worry caresses my cheek, but your lips, no
Windows are adorned with vases of sadness, but your flowers, no
My love, I've forgotten myself, I have no meaning
You're all that's left, are you absent, no

William Letford

ئەو لەمن ناچێ

ئاوێزان نوري حکیم

ئەو

پاییزێک رەنگی بردو

زەمەنێک پێتکەنینەکانی هەڵوەراند

شەوێک کردی بە پاڵەوانی شەقامە چۆڵەکان

ماڵێک خۆی پێ ئاوەدان کردەوە

ئێستائەو لە باوەشی کورسیەک

سەری ناوەتە سەر شانی مێزێک و

داوا لە مۆمێک دەکا جگەرەکە بۆ داگیرسێنێ

ئێستا ئەو لە نێو شیعرە زەردباوەکانی

بێدەنگیەکانی من و هاواری ئاوێنەکەی دەنوسێتەوە

کە پار ساڵ لە یادی لەدایکبونی پێی وتبوو

ئەی کەڵەگەترین غرور پیربونت باش

ئەو

مۆڵەتی لە حوزن وەرگرت و

پێنکی حەرفەکانی هەڵدا

مۆڵەتی لە شیعر وەرگرت و

ماڵێکی لە خەیاڵ چێکرد

مۆڵەتی لەمن وەرگرت و

باوەشی کرد بە مەراقێکی روتدا

بۆ شاردنەوەی دودڵیەکان

جگەرەیەکی خستە سەر لێو و.. من سوراوێک

ئەو رۆژنامەیەکی خوێندەوەوو من خەمەکانم راماڵی

ئەو مۆڕەی لێ کردم و من هێشتا سەمایەکی غەجەریانەی پێشکەش دەکەم

ئەو لەمن ناچێ

من مەریەمێکی سکپڕم بەهەناسەی تەنها پیاوێک

ئەو چەشنی عیسا

10

He's Not Like Me

Awezan Nouri Hakeem

Him?
Autumn bleached him out;
age withered his smile;
night made him Lord of all the empty streets
of his own home.
Now, foundering in his armchair,
he lays his head on the table's edge
and pleads with the candle to light his cigarette.
Somewhere deep in his washed-out verses
he transcribes my silences and the mirror's voice
that called out to him on his last birthday:
Hey, Mr Wonderful, Happy Old Age!
He asked Sadness to give him
back the words; asked Poetry
to build its little house of images;
asked my leave to throw himself
into Love's naked arms to soothe his pain.
He lifted a cigarette to his lips – I raised the lipstick to mine.
He read the Guardian; I swept my sadness under the rug.
I am Mary, heavy with the child of Man
And he's Jesus - virgins in their thousands follow him
to bow down before him, to trade their innocence
in the presence of his soul.
He's not like me.
He's sharper than granite when he tells me his hard luck stories.
He's hard as a pebble when he hurls himself at me

سەرنجی هەزاران راهیبەی راکێشاوە

تا لەبەردەم پیاوبوونیدا کرنۆش ببەن

تا لەبەردەم روحی ئەودا پاکیزەییان هەراج کەن

ئەو لەمن ناچێ

ئەو رەقتر لەبەرد دێته گۆ بۆ گێرانەوەی گەردی سەر روخسارو..

حیکایەتی شکاندن

ئەو توندتر لەبەرد خۆی دەگرێتە من

بۆ تەفسیرکردنی خەونی بن گۆمە ئاو و..

خەیاڵی زیخی نێو دەریا

ئەو زبتر بەخاک دەڵێ "من له جێ خۆم سەنگینترم" و

له "با" تیژتر پەنجەرەی قەدەر دەشکێنێ

ئەو دەیەوێ دەستەکانی بەراست و چەپ

چەشنی شەپۆل له نێو دەریای زەمەن مەله بکات و..

بمکێشێ به کەناری ئەجەلدا

تا مەرگێکی بەویقارم پێ ببەخشێ

ئەو هێشتاکە ئیرەیی بەخەندەکانم دەبات

نازانێ پاساریەک پێکەنینەکەی بەدرۆ خستەوە

ئەو لەمن ناچێ

من وەکو لاولاو

خۆم هەڵزنی به باڵای شیعرێکی و

بەر پەنجەرەی تەنیاییم به ئینجانەی عیشق رازاندەوەو

باخی غوربەتیم پرکرد له رەنگ

ئەو چەشنی پایز

ئالودەی هەڵوەرینە

دڵی سروشتم بۆ راگرت

نازی گەڵاکانیم هەڵگرت

له نێو باخچەی شیعر پیاسەم کردو..

به بەژنی گوڵێکی عەیار بۆنم کرد به حەرفەکانمەوە

هوتاف وەرینی دا به گوێیاند

to guddle meaning from the pool of my dreams
and inspiration from the shingles of the sea.
His is the flinty voice that tells the world: 'Wherever I am, I am the ballast';
keener than the gale that cracks Fate like a windowpane.
He's the swithering wave; he wants to flail his arms and swim through Time;
drag me behind him towards whatever fate I've earned;
grant me a fine death.
Even so, he envies me my smile;
he has no idea a sparrow gave away the secret: my happiness was a lie.
He's not like me –
sometimes he's a man of stone and sometimes water
wants to dye his loneliness the colour of me,
and frame me in exile,
hang me in a corner of his room
over those cracks doubt opened.
He throws me wild looks, curses my naked words.
He doesn't look like me. He doesn't look like himself.
He would envy the wind if it lifted my skirt
grow jealous of the water that wet my lips
He thinks it should only be him does that.
He's such a virtuoso on all my sadnesses:
when his fingers drift and dance like that.
Those eyes!
Such wild abandon!
He could play anything on me - any harmony.

John Glenday

ئەو لەمن ناچێ و

جارێک لە بەردو جارێکی دیکەش دەبێتە پیاوێک لە ئاو

لە باران دادەکاتە سەر حەسرەتەکانم

دەیەوێ تەنیاییەکانی بەمن رەنگ بکات

بمگریتە چوارچێوەی غوربەت و

لەبنمیچی ژوورەکەی هەڵمواسێ

لە درزی گومانەوە نیگای دۆزەخیم لێدەگرێ و

نەفرەت دەکات لە روتبونەوەی وشەکانم

ئەو لەمن ناچێ و لە خۆشی ناچێ

ئیرەیی بە (با) دەبات لە بری ئەو تەنورەم هەڵدەداتەوە

ئیرەیی بە (ئاو) دەبات لە بری ئەو لێوەکانم تەڕ دەکات

ئەو مایسترۆی ئازارەکانی منە

لەگەل جولّەی پەنجەکانی

چاوەکانی

سەرشێتیەکانی

بە ویستی خۆی دەمژەنێ.

إسق قلبي زهرة

صابرين كاظم

أليس أن ما يشرخ الحبيبين ... يورقهما؟
هو البعد هو التوهم
كنا الحديقة
انسفك علينا الضوء
و ترمد جمر الشعور.

صرنا عشبتين ضارتين،
لا نزهّر بعضنا ...

يُسلخ نسيج قلبي
و أنت لا تدري
أنام في الموت البطيء،
و تمرُّ
مثلَ من يكتب أبياتا من الشعر،

أو ما تدري؟
بأن الحب...
لنحياه

مثل هستيريا أيامنا مثل خلواتنا الخائفة
أو ما تدري بأن الصلاة
في مسجد الحبّ ملائكة ؟؟

يرشها العشاق بماء الورد
لينبتَ ورد
يبلوها بضوء الشمع

Water My Heart with a Jonquil

Sabreen Kadhim

So you think it's like the unspoken split
in the grafting of flowers,
both blooming brighter because of it?
That's only distance
wearing an intimate scent.

Our votive burns low—
we've learned to love each other
like we love ourselves, for ourselves
only, which, really, is no kind of love,
in the end. My heart is skinned raw.
And, don't you know, I sleep like the dead,
with the slowness of death, and here's you
writing your life with a hack's careless hand—
put that pen down and listen—love,
love is a poem, but it's also
the white space of mornings in bed,
it's the plink of the spoon at a café with friends.

Don't you know? That when you approach me, you come
as my penitent at the altar we cobbled, together?
That you carry in your pocket a vial of rosewater,
a candle to splash my floors with wax, with light,
your voice, like a glass of sweet wine?
And when your hands unfold from prayer,
it's not the wind that unfurls them, but you?

و الغناء الساكر؟

يداكَ مهبي
لا حفيف على سفن قلبك.

و الحب
المسافر
هو المسافر هو الوحي
ملائكته الشعور
انبياؤه الأيادي و القبل؟

يداك مهبي
و لا حفيف على سفن قلبك.

هو الحب مهبي...
أن تكتبَ علي يدي
إني احبكِ،
إني مهبتكَ
الريح

لا حفيف.

أهدني زهرة
قبل أن يفرغ قلبي
إسق قلبي زهرة. إفعل.

يداك مهبي، إفعل. طيّرهما
علق بالونا باسمي في نهارَك،
صر ضوئي مثل هذي السطور

That though you've barred your heart
love's revelation speaks
voicelessly, without cease,
like floodwaters building at your door,
and that the angels of the flood are also
the angels of what is between us?

Love is its own name on my hand in biro,
left there by your hand. It's jonquils nested in foil
to fill my bare garden table.
It's flying a balloon by a string from your window,
with my name shining across it.
It's you shining much like this string
of words across the page…that, that is love.

And again, I'll ask
how you can question it
and more, how can I possibly answer you?
Each time, I get out the thread, the needle,
to darn the tears on my heart,
but the stitches pull and lace together,
gathering tear to tear.
Are you awake? I am, though I've lost myself
in your dent in the sofa, so it's just
my body men see on the street.

And again, love is knowing my fingerprints,
your hands in my hair, your eyes
lighting my own like lamps in a window,

هو الحب مهبي،
و يداك القبل.

كيف احتجتَ إبرة السؤال؟
و كيف احتجتُ خيط الجواب؟
أخيط فتقي
أعود أخيط جرح الثوب، أبالغ أخيط و أبالغ
هذي الجروح فوق الجروح فوق الجروح
تشابكتْ،
تشابكت حتى الخيوط و ما التأمتُ

إنا لا أحلم،
أنا
أخيط
أخيط
و أخيط...
جرحي في نهارك،
جسدي هو الجرح.

الحب أن تلمس أطرافي
تهبط يداك على شِعري.
عيونك مصابيحي
تحتجب عن النعاس يدي
و تحسب المائدة المعتمة على يوم ضوء في البال.

أن نشعل كأسي شموع و نتدلى مثل النبيذ...
نسكر قبل النبيذ، ننعتق ننفتق، نغفى ثم نفيق.

never drawing the shades.
It's setting a place for two
when you meant to eat alone.
It's hanging vines in the garden with votives
and feeding each other light like grapes.
It's bringing me a dress to dance in,
knowing that I only own trousers.
It's playing together like children,
it's bending to my skinned knee.
It's growing me a jonquil. It's the surprise
on seeing your face at its center. Love
never knocks, nor does it live in our bed.
It makes its home in our eyes,
and shelters me from the wind.
It's the silent answer
to my silent question.
It's sewing me with kisses, like seeds…

So, has the wick blackened to its end
or was it simply never lit?
Are you with me? Are you with me?
Don't you dare ask me back…I'm here,
clutching my match in the darkness.

Krystelle Bamford

أن تلبسني إرجواناً لنرقص،
أن نلعب (ختيلة...)
سأخرقُ اللعبة أمسكني.

أن تحضّر الزهرةَ و حديقتي الى قلب السفينة
الحب ذات المسافرة،
هو أن اللهفة تقدح العيون
على صدر السفينة.

يُخرج التائه خيباتي
و يرتق فتق الأسئلة

ما صار كل ذلك...
هل حصل؟

أستدرجني إلى سرير غيابك،
لأحرق كل الغياب... كلَّ آثاث الغياب
لا تحترق، إحرق البداية
احرق الباب.
على باب السفينة احترق...
احترق المسافرون و بضاعة الحب

ما كدت أقدح شمع المواعيد حتى ذوت...

يا لهذا العذاب المتعَب المتشبث الخائف.

سرطان

كريستال بامفورد

لو رسمتَ خارطةً لنجدها
تلك الزهور المظلمة و هي تتفتحُ في أعماقِكَ
قُل : موافق
لأكونَ لِصّةَ أوركيد
أدخلُ و في كفّي مجرفة
و حذائي طويلٌ كحذاء بُستاني
حشائشُكَ يلظمُها الماءُ المالح
و أنا أتموّجُ مع أهوار "فلوريدا"
لأجمعَ شباكَ المرض ... أقتلعها
و يدي تفيضُ بالأرجوان

ستتبقى واحدةٌ ... أُسميها الزهرةَ الصلعاءَ ... تويجاتها تلهثُ بالأصفر
ستكون حينَ أعودُ ... علامة النصر
تلك التي أسرتها ... زهرة السلام و السكون
و إصبعي الوسطى في وجه ما تبقى.

زاهر موسى

Cancer

Krystelle Bamford

Draw us a map and we will find them,
those dark, sudden flowers.

Give me leave and I will go in
with waders, a spade—an orchid thief

piloting the mangrove, the tangled, brackish
backwaters. I will root them all out

and return with just one— a perfect,
pale head, a yellow tongue. We will call

this thing the flower of peace, of silence,
of leave us fucking be.

ولد ليموت

زاهر موسى

أبلغِ اللهَ أنَّ المرايا نجومٌ في ليلِ الفقراء
و أنَّ نهاراتِهم تُلعقُ في النوافذ
و أبلغهُ ... أنَّ الشحاذين أرصفة
و أنَّ المتقاعدين يعملون ...
و أنَّ الأطبّاء ينظرون إلى ساعاتهم في العمليات
و يستخدمون الآلة الحاسبة
و أبلغهُ أنَّ المدينةَ تفلّي شيبَ شوارعها من المارّة
و أنَّ البلادَ أسرةٌ مهاجرةٌ تركبُ قطارَ الصدفةِ و حقائبها الوهم ...
و أبلغهُ أنَّ بيتَ أبيكَ و جدَّكَ لا يتسعُ للبكاء الذي يسمعُ خارجهُ
فكيف سيتسعُ للناس ؟...
و أنَّ غرفةَ أمّكَ يخبزُ حيطانها الوقتُ
أرغفةً للانتظار ...

و أبلغهُ أنَّكَ مررتَ سريعاً على الحياةِ
حتى أنَّكَ تركتَ بكائك في أُذنِ المستشفى
و أنَّكَ فوّتَ على نفسكَ
غيمةً في سماء امّكَ تُسمّى الحضن
و مهداً تهزّهُ الريحُ لولدها الفراغ ...
و يدَ والدكَ الخاليةَ منك ...
و أنَّكَ فوّتَ لقاءَ(عمر السراي و جاسم بديوي و احمد عبد السادة و سام محمود و علي وجيه و مؤيد الخفاجي)*
و قراءةَ (سركون بولص و رعد عبد القادر و دنيا ميخائيل و جمال جاسم أمين و مروان عادل حمزة)*
و كان ذلك سيعجبك ...
و أبلغهُ أنَّ الكلماتِ تتختّرُ في الأفواه
و أنَّ الإشاراتِ تكسّرُ الأيدي
و أنَّ اللغةَ تكتبُ بالأبيض

Born to Die

Zaher Mousa

Tell God, mirrors are the stars of the poor
because they see nothing but good in the mirror's inversion

And that when the afternoon light hangs in their windows, they lick it
because the poor are that thirsty for light

And tell him the road is paved with beggars
And that those who had retired have to keep on working...

While even as they operate, surgeons watch the clock
and calculate how long they can give each patient.

Tell him, Baghdad plucks its people like grey hairs from its streets
and that all of a sudden,

like a family throwing its possessions into a couple of hastily-packed bags,
Iraq doesn't know where it's going.

And tell him, "the house of my father and my grandfather is so small
that the people on the street can hear them crying through the walls,

so how would it ever have accommodated our whole family?"
And "my mother watched the clock for nine months for nothing, watched

while time baked it like a flat-bread – but who can eat a clock?"
And tell him your life passed so quickly

و تقالُ بالصمتِ ...

و أبلغهُ أنَّ الجميعَ أطلّوا من زجاجِ قلبك
و أشاروا إلى عدم اكتمالك
رغم أنَّ الإنسانَ ناقصٌ دائما
و الكمالُ لك وحدكَ ...
و أبلغهُ أنَّ ...

* أصدقاء الشاعر
* شعراء يكتبون قصيدة نثر حقيقية

that even as you stand before God
your cry is still ringing in the hospital's ear

And that you missed your chance to be cradled
like a cumulus in the sky of your mother's arms

And that you left your father's cupped hands empty

And ask him "Who lies in the cradle now?
Does the wind rock his own child?"

And tell him "I never got to meet Omar al-Saray, Jasim Bidiwi, Ahmad
    Abd al-Sada,
Sam Mahmoud, Ali Wajih and Mu'eed al Khafaji

Or to read Sargon Boulus, Ra'd abd al Qadir, Dina Mikha'il, Jamal Jasim
    Amin,
and Marwan 'Adil Hamza

And I would've liked to."

And say that words thicken in the mouths of the Iraqis
and the arms that dare to gesture are broken

And that language writes white
And speaks silence

And tell him that when our friends first saw you in the incubator, they said –
he'll never make it, his heart is half-grown

But we are all universally imperfect
And wholeness, perfection

These are yours alone

And tell him…
tell him…

Jen Hadfield

توديع
كريستال بامفورد

بعضهم يغادر عبر البنفسج
آخرون عبر ستارة الباب
بعضهم يملك شيئاً
في الجيب – مثلاً
ورقة الرهان
اذا كان ممن يفضلون
الكلاب السلوقية.

هل سترحل في قارب؟
ماذا ستعتقد
عندما لا يُبلل الماء
حافة بنطلونك، عندها تدرك أن خوفك منه
قد انتهى؟

بعضهم يغادر عبر أزهار عرف الديك،
أو القلب المُدَّمَى
أو لا تنساني.
لا يهم.

بعضهم يملك شيئاً
في الجيب
لما بعد. إذهب
عبر النافذة
لمرة واحدة في حياتك
سأحملُ رأسَك
اذا ما حمل آخر
قدميك.

غريب اسكندر

Wake

Krystelle Bamford

Some go in violets.
    Others through the screen door.
Some have something
    in the pocket—say,
        a racing slip
        if they loved
        the greyhounds
        best.

Will you travel by boat?
    What will you think
        when the water won't wet
        your cuffs, when you find
        your fear
            of water is gone?

Some go in cock's comb,
    bleeding heart,
    forget-me-not.
    It doesn't matter.
Some have something
    in the pocket,
    for later. Go

through the window
for once in your life.
I'll cup your head
if someone
takes your heels.

ما وراء فيزاليوس

جون غلانداي

في فصوله السبعة عن نسيج الجسم البشري
أراني فيزاليوس رجلاً من الأموات
يستعرضُ اذرعاً مقشرة بانتشاء
تتدلى عضلاتها الصلدة من الرسغين
كحصّالاتِ نقودٍ يملؤها الدم
ما وراؤهُ حقولٌ ...
كلّما أنضجتها خطوات الزمن المتباعدة
تضاءلت شمسها و الغيوم
و ارتفعت أبراج قرى بين التلال
كتلك التي على علبة الشوكولاته

***

و نحن ... كرجل فيزاليوس ...
لا ندركُ شبه موتينا
"شبه كلامنا الأفقي و فكرتنا التي بلا قعر و تقاليدنا الفارعة"
و رغم أنها تسلُّ مذاكيرنا صعوداً للّسان ...
هذه الأرض
سننغرسُ حتى الرُكب
و رغم ما تبقى من دواخل نابضةِ اللحم
تمنيناها لبّاً يُطلُّ على العالمِ بعُريه المُفصّص
كذلك هو الحبُّ أو الضيم.

زاهر موسى

After Vesalius

John Glenday

Among the illustrations in Vesalius' *De Humani Corporis Fabrica*
I saw a dead man lift up in wonder his marvellous, flayed hands.
Fibres of raw muscle hung from both wrists, as heavy as purses
filled with blood. Behind him fields ripened slowly, little weathers grew,
and the spires of his village rose between chocolate-box hills.

Although we also must seem dead, in a manner of speaking,
(our breadth of speech, depth of thought, length of custom)
we will stand rooted to this country which has gouged us crotch
to tongue, with all those inner workings we had hoped would let us move
resected and laid bare. Such is the case in agony or love.

Like a Smoored Ember

يبقى على تلك الجذوة

From 'The Session'
(Jen Hadfield/ Ghareeb Iskander)
Kufic Calligraphy by Samir Sumaida'ie

جلسة موسيقية

جين هادفيلد

حلقة رجال
تنحني ظهورهم
على قيثاراتهم
ينظرون فقط الى بعضهم البعض
أو بعبارة اكثر دقة
ينظر بعضهم الى جفون البعض الآخر
كما شاشات موقد
جلد حيوان موحل
حيث بصمات أياد وسحرة بدائيين
تقافز رجال
وهرولاتهم مع خنازير برية.

اللحن
هذا الشيء يعتنون به
قصاصات دي-أن-أي اللدنة
وعلى أحدهم
أن يثابر
كي يبقي على تلك الجذوة
في مخبئه الجلدي
الى قادمين آخرين
ليعتنوا بها
في قرفصاتهم
ويهيموا بها
بجهد شديد
فهذا اللهيب الطحلبي من لوازمها.

The Session

Jen Hadfield

A ring of men
doubled over
the bellyache
of their guitars
looking at anything
but each other
but mostly
at firescreens
of eyelids –
muddy hide
where's patterned
handprints and gravied
shamans and leaping
and running men
and boars.
The tune's the thing
they're nursing,
a malleable scrap
of DNA
one nominate
must bear
in a hide pouch
like a smoored
ember
to the next camp
where they'll squat

وعلى هذه الشاكلة يقتات لحن على آخر

وهكذا الى لحن آخر

على طول الأيام اللاحقة

ليبني بلا حدود

من الموسيقى

بيتا دائرياً

دونما أي باب.

غريب اسكندر

on it and fan
for dear life
its fitting,
mossy flame.
Subsisting tune
to tune like this
through the later days,
infinitely bigging
the roundhouse
of music
with no door.

notes: *bigging* – building; *moored* – smothered

فاصلة

صابرين كاظم

لنْ يَقولَ لكَ أحدٌ ذلك:
ستجدُ النّدمَ خلفَ مقبضِ البابِ،
لنْ ينوهَ لكَ أحدٌ بذلك:
أنّكَ في الخارجِ،
رغم شعورِك
بأنّكَ علامة فارقة
مثل (*) على الهامش
أكثرُهم بلاغةً لنْ يفعل!!
...

لن يُخرجَ أحدٌ أحشاءَ ماضيهِ
ليقذفَها في سلّتِك ...
كي يتخلصَ من الذاكرة على الاقلِّ،
لن يتوقفَ أحدُهم عندكَ طويلاً
أو يتكئ
لن ينتظرَعندَكَ أو معكَ
لأنّكَ لستَ كرسيّاً ببساطةٍ!
لن يهشَّ أحدٌ الطنينَ عن قلبِكَ

هذا لأنّكَ لم تكنْ باصا أو محطة
لستَ شارعاً أو جسراً
لستَ رصيفاً أو شجرةً

تقفُ على قدمٍ واحدةٍ
تنتظرُ زائرَكَ طويلاً
تفتحُ له ذراعاً
فينفلتُ منكَ مسرعاً

Comma

Sabreen Kadhim

No one will let you in on this:
that what lies beyond that door is regret

no one will explain that you're the outsider
despite your conviction that you're the defining feature –

you languish
like a footnote

at the bottom of the page
that you'd need a scholar to decipher
but even the scholars aren't letting on!

No-one is giving anything away.
No-one will offer you the benefit of his experience
or unburden himself to you
no-one will linger to get this off her chest
or put her feet up or wait along with you

because what you are not
is a chair!

The thoughts that drone like flies about you
no-one will dispel

because you are not a bus or a station

و قد تُصابُ بجرحٍ إثر ذلك
أو قد تتخشبُ أكثر

دائـما يظنّون بكَ السوء
يتهمونك بالبرود و السذاجة،
أو يتعاملون معكَ مثل خادمٍ مطيعٍ

كلما خرجتْ منكَ حقيبةٌ
وددتَ لو أنّكَ ثياب
كلما شممتَ عطرا
وددتَ لو أنك رائحة

لن يقول لكَ أحدٌ ذلك:
ستجدُ النّدمَ خلفَ مقبضِ الباب،
كلّ هذا من أجلكَ
لن ينوهَ أحدٌ لكَ به
أكثرُهم بلاغةً لنْ يفعل
بأنّكَ علامةٌ فارقةٌ
مثل (*) على الهامش
هذا ببساطةٍ
لأنّكَ باب!

or a road or a bridge
or a pavement or a tree
so you stand on one leg
looking forward to your visitor

and you sweep your welcoming arm open –
just for him to give you the slip
and escape your embrace.

So you toughen up –
wounded, wooden,
primitive, slavish

this is what they say about you.

Somebody is coming…wearing perfume.
If only you were perfume.

Somebody passes through you with a suitcase.
How you wish you were clothes.

No-one will tell you
that regret is what lies beyond that door –
no-one will say "I'm telling you this
for your own good."

You're so scholarly, and so inarticulate!
Like the footnote languishing
in the page's gutter.

And they will never tell you
because you are simply
a door!

Jen Hadfield

أمي، بابا ياغا*

كريستال بامفورد

إذا أسقطت مشطها البلاستيكي، المشط الذي
تسرح به خصلات شعرها الفضية كل يوم قبل العمل،
تقول الحكايات الشعبية أن الغابة المتشابكة تتفتح، و كل
الألحية السود، و تربة الطين الخصبة التي تشبه القار، كلها تنفتح إن حركته

الى حديقتها الغامضة، إن كانت تعرف الأسماء
للأعشاب الملتفة، و العنكبوت الأحمق هذا
الذي يسمى وحيد و أرمل، بيتها الخشبي
ستنمو له ساقان طويلتان، و هي حتما ستغادر

لنا، نحن و شتاؤنا المالح، كلنا غادرتنا وراءها. في كل عيد ميلاد رأس السنة
ربما تتسنى لنا زيارة الأطلال... نتعجب كم أنها ضخمة
آثار أقدام رحيلها، الفسطون* العاري من الزهر،
نلمسه مع خيوط شعرها الفضية مثل التينسال*.

يقولون
لا يوجد نظام في بيت بلا إمرأة.
و أنا أقول
كلوا الأطفال، خذوا المنزل معكم، أديروا ظهوركم
و غادروا

صابرين كاظم

* بابا ياغا: ساحرة في الحكايات الشعبية بيتها له أرجل تشبه أرجل الدجاجة، تتنقل عبره، تأوى الأطفال
المشردين و اليتامى فيه، و إذا جاعت تأكلهم
* الفسطون: حبل من الزهور تزين به البيوت في عيد الميلاد
* التينسال: الخيوط الملونة التي تزين بها شجرة الميلاد

My Mama, Baba Yaga

Krystelle Bamford

If she dropped her plastic comb, the one she threads
with silver hairs each morning before work,
the folktales say a wood will bloom, all thick,
black bark and loam like bitumen. If she tended

to her own dark garden, if she knew the names
of the herbs that coil and the spider that fools
call *recluse* or *widow*, her clapboard house
would grow long legs, and she would leave

us, our salted winters, all behind. Each Christmas
we could visit the foundation and marvel at how huge
the footprints of her leaving, and festoon the bare
concrete with silver hairs, like tinsel. They say

there is no order in a house without a woman. I say eat
the children, take the house, turn your back, and go.

هێدرا

جین هادفێلد

ئایا ئێمه له خاکناسهکان دهچوین
یان ئهوان له ئێمه
کاتێ پێکهوه له باخچهکه
بهریزبهندی زهویهکهمان دهکێلا
به ههموو بازوهکانمانهوه
خۆڵهکانمان ههڵدهگێڕایهوه
جاروباریش
دهکهوتینه نێو ئیقاعێکی مهزنهوه
له ژێر پێیهکان سهری خاکناسهکان دهلهرینهوه
کاتێک تۆ گۆشهی پارچهیهک له زهوی دهبڕی
ههموو پێکهوه له درزی زهویهکهدا موسهکانمان ههڵگرت و
قورسیهکی مردومان ههڵگهڕانهوه
وهکو ئهوهی کێشی خاک هانمان بدات
ههموو پێکهوه به ههمان پارچه زهویمان کێشاو ههڵمانگێڕایهوه
لهگهڵ ئهوهی خاکناسهکان به دریژایی زهمهن ئاڵتر دهبونهوه
چهشنی سهری کۆبرا له ههمان گرێی بازووهوه هێش دهبهن
سێ چاوی کول تیشکدانهوهی ههتاو
دهستم بهر شانی یهکیان دهکهوت و
رۆخی کلاوهکانیش چهشنی جاز بهر یهک دهکهوتن
دهستێک بۆ دهرهێنانی گۆوگیایهک دریژبوو
لهولاتر خاکناسێک هێشی هێنا
ههندێ جاریش روو له دورگهی فیۆلا ی بهتهمی شین داپۆشراوو
پشویهکی تر به ههناسه بڕکێوه بهرازهکانمان فێنک دهکردهوه
بهرازهکان بهخۆراتهکاندن پروشهی موه زبرهکانیانهوه
گوتیهکانیان چهشنی گهڵای لههانه
لهخۆشیدا بهدهوری لانهکانیان سهمایان دهکرد

Hydra

For D, S & F; A & L
Jen Hadfield

Were we like a plough, ancient or modern,
or a plough like us

as we laboured together along the rows
and down the yard,

straining to turn the chunked soil,
and intermittently fell into a genius rhythm:

in unison trod
the spade-heads, and teetered

while you cut
the corner of the clod;

and raised our blades
in the fissure to turn the dead

weight of it together
and then, impelled by momentum

and gravity, struck
the same, rolled clod in unison

with spades honed over the years

کڵاوەکانمان لە ئاو پڕکردو
گەڕاینەوە لای خاکناسەکان بە چۆڕانەوەی دڵۆپە ئاوەکان
بەسەر گوێیەکانماندا
ئەوکاتانە خۆر زەوییە هەڵگێڕدراوەکانی تینو دەکرد
تا کۆتا... تا ئاوابوونی.

ئاوێزان نوری حکیم

to a thin, ragged edge,
as cobra-heads with hoods spread
dash from the same knot

of muscle; three dull eyes
blanking the sun?
Just as often I whacked one of you

with my hip or arse
or our hat-brims cymballed

or the spade just missed the hand
that darted into turned earth

for lim or plumped, pale mandrakes
of docken root,

or we eyed Foula
distant in blue haze

and panted, or hosed the pig,
who shuddered the bright water

from her curling bristles
and her loud ears like cabbage leaves,

and in an eruption of the spirit
tacked about her park.

Or we filled our hats at the tap
and worked on with earlobes dripping

while the dryness washed down
from our first row,

the turned roots
parching in the sun,

until it was done,
in the cooling of the light.

notes: *Foula* – an island to the west of Shetland (pronounced /fulˈə/); *lim* – pieces of broken china

تماثيل الذهن

ويليام لتفورد

حول طاولة المطبخ يجلسُ ثلاثة رجال. جدي

يدخن غولدن فرجينيا. حيثُ لفُ سيجارة صار شعيرةً له.

فأصابعه تساعده على التفكير، هذا هو عمله.

حينما تفوح رائحة التبغ من علبته.

أبي يدخن سِلِك گَت

وله طريقته في مسكها

يوقعها في شرك اصبعيه الأولين

يرفعها من ثم الى فمه ويترك يده تغطي الجزء الأسفل

من وجهه.

أما أنا فلستُ مدخناً

لكنَّ الرجلين يستمتعان بطريقة تناولي الشوربة

عمرا دخان

دنسا غرفة لم تكن

مع أنها المكان الذي ارتاده بحثاً عن نصيحة ما.

أصفع ملعقتي على الطاولة

حسنٌ، إذا كان الأمر هكذا، إن الأمر هكذا

"الأمر هكذا". يقول جدي

بينما يومئ أبي برأسه قائلاً

"إن الأمر هكذا"

غريب اسكندر

Monuments of the Mind

William Letford

Three men sit at the kitchen table. My grandfather
smokes Golden Virginia. Making a roll up
has become his ritual. His fingers help him think
So that's what he does. He teases tobacco from his tin
My father smokes Silk Cut and has a certain way
of holding a cigarette. Trapping it at the base
of his first two fingers and lifting it to his mouth
so his hand covers the lower half of his face. I don't smoke
but there is a bowl of soup in front of me. Both men
like to see me eat. The room has been stained
with two lifetimes of tobacco smoke, and doesn't
physically exist. But it's where I come for advice. In fact
both men no longer exist, but their voices are as familiar
as my own failings. I slam my spoon onto the table
Well if that's the way it is then that's the way it is
'That's the way it is,' says my grandfather
My father nods his head. He says, 'that is the way it is.'

البيت و العائلة

زاهر موسى

البيت

بيتنا بسمةٌ كاذبة
تئنُّ أبوابهُ كأنكَ تدخلُ جرحا
و أطفالنا
قشورُ فواكه

الزجاجُ ماءٌ مندهش
و النافذةُ شلالٌ محنط
و نساؤنا خشنات
كيدِ مزارع

السلمُ ظهرٌ مكسور
و السقفُ نتناوب و الجدران على حمله
و شبابنا رئة من لهاث

الغرفُ داكنٌ سرّها
كموعدٍ ليلي
و الأسرّة
تنامُ حينَ نصحو
متعبةً من تقلّبنا المرير
و أمّنا ليلةٌ في النهار
و نهارٌ في الليل

المكتبةُ زحامٌ مثقف
و الكمبيوتر سائحٌ تائه
و أبونا في الصورةِ
يشعرُ بالمللِ من الموت.

The House and the Family

Zaher Mousa

The House

Our house stands like a smile, but it's false
The door groans like a slow wound
and children scatter like peels of fruit in a draft

A glass on the table is perfectly startled
The living room window is a waterfall stilled
It's like one moment of sky. The women
that pass from room to room are as
beautiful and tough as the hands of a farmer

Our staircase is back broken
it's like the walls are so weak
we must hold up the ceiling
The young are breathless beneath this roof

Our bedrooms are dusty with shadows and secrets
Tired from turning they sleep when we wake
Our mother is clothed like the moon in the morning
and sheds her abaya like a sunrise at night

Our library is respectable, it's cultured, it's charming
The computer is lonely, it's a foreigner, it's lost
Our father in his picture
Is bored of death

العائلة

أطفالنا عضة في حلمة

و أبوابنا تُجذفُ في الريح

و البيتُ مرساتهُ في القلب

نساؤنا يشتعلن قبل النار

و حينَ ينضجُ الأكل

يدخلن سنِّ اليأس

و النوافذُ جارحةٌ دونَ أنْ تنكسر

شبابنا عازبون عن العمل و عاطلون عن الزواج

و بثورهم بعددِ أحلامهم الشبقة

و السقفُ منعَ القمرَ من رؤيتنا

فأضاءَ السلم

أمّنا ترتدي حزنها

و تراهنُ شيبتها

على الاسوداد

و الأسرّةُ مائدة النوم

و الغرفةُ وطنٌ بسريرين

أبونا لم يغادر الإطار منذ أنْ ولد

و حتى بعد أنْ مات وطنياً

و الكمبيوتر كمبيوتر

لم يتصنع الذكاء

و لم يتذاك صناعياً

و حيثُ سجنَ الصمتُ الكلامُ تكون المكتبة.

The Family

Our doors open like oars in the wind
Our babies are salt spray and teeth marks on nipples
This house has laid anchor in our hearts

Our young women flare like flames on a stove
and age before the water has boiled
Some windows can become scars on the world

Our young men, divorced from work
Shuffle in the dole queue of love
ambition and tenderness
have become wet dreams and acne

Our room is a world
Where unmade beds are banquets of sleep
My mother's hair is too bright for her grief
She dies it black

Our computer is solid and assure of its logic
and our father was a man that lived by his rules
War gave him new rules, and a frame he'll never leave
Our library is as silent as a prison of speech

William Letford

العِبرة

ويليام لتفورد

مُصاباً بالربو تتأرجحُ حبالهُ الصوتية،
ذلك الطفل،
بينَ رئتيه، شاهقةً تتدلى
يتكئُ بينَ زفيرٍ وآخر،
مُتذكراً تقويمَ الهواءِ في صدره
و اهتزازَ الأشياءِ من الداخل.
ذلك الطفل،
تمسُ كتفَهُ الأمُ و هي في طريقها إلى التذاكر و الفشار و الكولا و أصابعها تتقارب عند نهاياتِ رأسهِ البنية.
ذلك الطفل،
يلتقطُ الأشياءَ بعينيه، عيناهُ واسعتا البريق
لو أنّه نظرَ عالياً
لانسكبتْ المجرّاتُ فيهما.

زاهر موسى

Wisdom

William Letford

The boy has asthma. His wheeze is somewhere
between a moan and a whistle, and there is a
pause before each intake, as if it's necessary
to concentrate, to think, breathe. The mother
talks, asking for tickets, and popcorn, and cola
She grips his shoulder, and touches
the back of his head. All the while the boy
is watching, and his eyes are electric. They are
wonderful. Big enough so that, if he wanted to
he could tip his head back and pour the world in.

Their Women are Perfumed Sadnesses

نساؤهم حزن معطر

From 'The Iraqi Elements'
(Zaher Mousa/ John Glenday)
Kufic Calligraphy by Samir Sumaida'ie

البتولا و القيقب

جين هادفيلد

بعضنا أشجار بتولا و قيقب، لا يلزمهم أحسان ليبكون. يرشح الدمع، دمعهم، دون ملاحظة أحد. الدمع جذر ملتو، يلج بشهوة بئر الأذن. و عصير البتولا مطلقاً، يغلي لينتج الشحة، شحة الدمع أو الى لا شيء فقط.

آخرون مجدبون، يمطرون بمشقة؛ الهواء و طبقات الجلد العلوية، أبويهما، يتصارعان لتبني كل دمع مكثفة تسقط، بكاؤهم، مثل حلب النعاج، يلزمه وقتا و هلاكاً، مثل حصد الزعفران، أو كما تقضم نباتات آكلة للحوم ندى.

صابرين كاظم

Birches and Maples

Jen Hadfield

Some of us are birches and maples, and don't need any help to cry. They weep without noticing. A tear is a twisted root, shoved lustily into the ear. And the syrup of the fluent birch boils down to next-to-nothing.

Others are arid. They wetten with effort; air and skin tussle for custody of each concentrated tear. Crying them is as time-consuming as milking ewes, as harvesting saffron, or the carnivorous plant's sparse dews.

خەریکە کاڵ دەچمەوە

ئاویزان نوري حکیم

ئەو کاتەنای
گوڵێک خەریکە دەخنکێ
سۆزی باران لەکوێیه
گەڵایەک خەریکە دەمرێ
ئامێزی (با) له کوێیه
ژنێک خەریکه دەکوژرێ
شەرەفی پیاوێک له کوێیه
ئاڵایەک گەر بسوتێرێ
حزوری نیشتمان کوێیه

Fading

Awezan Nouri Hakeem

When a flower dies
Where is the passion of rain

When a leaf dies
Where is the embrace of the wind

When a woman is killed for honour
Where is the dignity of man

When a flag is burned
Where is the conscience of a country

William Letford

الطبائع العراقية الأربع

زاهر موسى

في الأول من مائهم ...

تشعرُ بأجنّةِ المطر تموتُ في البخار

و الأنهارُ تغرقُ في الموتِ و الضفاف و الكسل

و في الصنابيرِ تسمعُ أصواتَ الهاربين من العطش ..

و تقرأ على زيرهم ... " اشربْ الحسين و تذكرْ عطشَ الماء"

(آباؤهم) ... ظمأ طريّ / رملٌ ممزوجٌ بالدم

(آباؤهم) ... دوارٌ صلب / رحىّ تطحنُ السراب

خرجوا للحرب و حين عادوا لم يجدوا ما يتوضأون به فتيمموا المقبرة

و في الأول من هوائهم ...

تشعرُ بزفيرِ الملائكةِ المتعبين و غلاصمِ الجنِّ في معابرِ السماء

و تشمُّ رائحةً عيونهم التي ترى من داخل النار أوردة الغيب

و تلمسُ رئاتَ الزنازين التي تنفست شبابهم المدفون ...

نساؤهم ... حزنٌ معطر / كحلٌ و دمع في عربة الريح

نساؤهم ... غربةٌ ملونة / ملابسٌ سوداء في حقائبَ ضائعة

راهن التنورُ على أرغفة وجوههنّ فكسِبتْ الحرب

و حين انتهتْ ,, تنفسنَ أجنحةً الغربان و مراوح الغرف الضيقة

و في الأولِ من نارهم ...

تشعرُ باهتزاز الشظايا في ظهور العائدين من الخنادق

و احتراق السجائرِ في جيبِ مدخنٍ أصبح سيجارةً للموت

و حرارة الأورامِ و هي تنمو في رؤوس الأطفال

أطفالهم ... ضحكٌ مرسوم / أوراقُ لعبٍ لا تحتمل الجوكر

أطفالهم ... جمالٌ مفتَّت / خبزٌ تُغمّسهُ الحياةُ في الطرقاتِ عصرا

The Iraqi Elements

Zaher Mousa

This is the birth of Water:

Mist is when water dies so that it can be born again.

Sluggish rivers swither among the dead, their banks overflowing.

Listen: those whisperings in the pipework are all the refugees from thirst.

The inscription on the fountain's cup reads:

'Drink, Hussain, and remember thirst.'*

Their fathers: their fathers' gentle thirst, as if sand were slowly pouring
   into blood;

light-headed as a stone, as the millstone that wears its mirage back to sand.

So they went off to war and when they came back, no water for the ritual
   cleansing,

not one drop, so they washed themselves in graveyard dust.

*****

This is the birth of Air:

Weary angels revel in it: the sky is laced with the gutturals of genies;

those fragrant eyes that glimpse the invisible smouldering in their veins.

Here you touch against breasts that breathed in childhood's loss.

Their women: their women are like perfumed sadnesses; their gaze carried
   away on the wind

bleached of all colour: their black clothes abandoned - still in suitcases
   somewhere.

The women wagered on hard graft and the smoking tanur, their faces tender
   as the good bread;

و لأطفال العالم كراتٌ يلعبون بها , أما هم فلم يكن لهم كرات
إذ كانت رؤوسهم هي كرات الآخرين   ...

و في الأولِ من ترابهم ...
تشعرُ بالتراب.

but War won that bet, of course. War always does.
And when it was all over they breathed in. They breathed in the soot of a
    crow's wing;
the drift of fans through narrow rooms.

*****

This is the birth of Fire:
Soldiers trudge home from the front line. Slivers of shrapnel glimmer
    inside them.
Here's a dead man with a cigarette in his pocket, still alight – his last smoke.
Cancers flare and smoulder deep in the heads of children.
Their children: their children with happiness chalked into their faces –
if they were a pack of playing cards, there wouldn't be any joker.
Their children are little chunks of the good bread, dunked in muddy
    kerbside puddles:
Life will gobble them up.
In other countries children have footballs to play with, but not here,
no, in this country they used the children's heads as footballs.

*****

This is the birth of Earth:
Feel this: feel the earth.

John Glenday

notes: *tanur* – wood-fired oven
*Originally: 'Drink the water, and remember Hussain'.

من أجل الرحلة

ويليام لتفورد

لم يقل كلمةً، عندما أخبروه عن الذي يقبع تحت الصخر

وضع جبهته فقط عليه، ثم وضع يداً واحدة، اثنتين

وانطلق للعمل. لم ير أحدٌ من الرجال

شخصاً يائساً على هذه الشاكلة عندما أضاءت مصابيح خوذاتهم ظهره

الذي تحرك وشب لكنه لم ينحرف. شاهدوه وهو يغوص بقدميه في الوحل. يحل الصمت حينما يتعب

ليأخذ نفساً ويعود الى العمل. علينا أن نوقفه

قال أحد الرجال. دعه وشأنه، قال آخر، أو وإلّا لن يعرف أنه يستحيل عليه رفعه.

غريب اسكندر

For the Journey

William Letford

When they told him who was beneath the boulder, he didn't say a word
just placed his forehead against it, then one hand, then two
then set his shoulder to work. None of the men had seen someone so
desperate, so methodical. The lamps on their helmets brightened his back
that shifted and bucked but wouldn't buckle. They watched as his boots
dug troughs in the dirt. Whenever he tired there'd be silence
then three deep breaths and he would go again. We should stop him
said one man. Leave him, said another, or he'll never know he couldn't lift it.

أفعـى گلگامـش

غريب اسكندر

أغنيـة

غنّى كلَّ شيء

غنى الأرصفة النائمة

والفجر الغريب

غنى روحه وجسده

حبيبته وأمه

غنى الملائكة والشياطين

غنى الربيع

الأزهار التي تنمو

من بعد ليل طويل

غنى الشوارع

لم يغن الجدران

غنى

وغنى

وغنى

غنى بعينيه

وبيديه

وبقلبه

لم يغن بفمه

كان صمته أبلغ أغنية

كانت حياته

رقصة موت

وأيامه

فراغاً هامساً.

Gilgamesh's Snake

Ghareeb Iskander

Song

He sang the sum of things:
the drowsing pavement,
the unfamiliar dawn.
He sang his soul and body.
His lover and his mother.
He sang angels, he sang devils.

He sang Springtime -
the flowers which open themselves
after a long night.
He sang the streets
but he wouldn't sing the hindering walls.

He sang
and he sang
and sang.

He sang with his eyes
and with his hands.
He sang with his heart
but his mouth did no singing.
The richest of all his songs was silence.
His life was
death's little dance

گلگامش

كلكامش
وحيد الآن
يغطيه الثلج
يتقاسمه الموج
تلفه الحشائش
يستنجد بالعشب
لكن
لا أحد هناك
يسمعه
فأوروك خاوية
لا أحد فيها
يلفها الصمت
شوارعها خاوية
يمشي فيها وحيداً
لا أشجار تستظل بها روحه الهائمة
لا كأس تطفئ غربته
يبكي وحيداً
ولأن انتصاره كان هزيمة دائمة
ظل طوال عمره
يمتطي سعفة من نخيل
يمشي في شوارع أوروك
يقابل اناساً غرباء
سحنتهم سحنته
أسماؤهم تشبه اسمه
لكنهم
غرباء
غرباء
في هذه البلاد الغريبة.

and his days all
emptiness - a whispering void.

Gilgamesh
Gilgamesh.
He's alone now.
Snow covers him.
He's all at sea.
Swaddled in lushness,
he looks to the grass of life for help
but
there's no one there
to hear him.
Uruk is an empty ruin,
all its people fled.
Such devastation; the streets
shimmer in a caul of silence.
He wanders alone -
not a single tree shades his scorched soul,
no wine to quench his longing.
All alone, he cries,
and because victory for him is a defeat that never ends
till the ends of his life, he must
ride the magic palm frond.
He walks the streets of Uruk,
meets strangers
who look like him,
their names like his name
but

أيها السيد

يحرقني هذا الضوء

هذه الموسيقى القادمة

من آفاق الروح

يحرقني هذا الأمل الكاذب

هذا الجسد الذي يحترق

هذه المرايا التي لا تشير الى شيء

تحرقني هذه العتمة

لا شيء هناك

لا شيء

ارحلْ عنها

لا تعد اليها

ربما لا تنتهي هذه القصيدة.

خاتمة

لم يكن قد رأى

أي شيء

كانت النهاية فقط

ما يُحيط به

لا أبراج

لا سلام

ولا حتى أغنية

يغنيها في تلك الوحشة

حلق عالياً

وبعدما أصبح قاب قوسين

أو أدنى من أحلامه البعيدة

تدلى

بقوة

نحو

القصيدة.

they are strangers.
Strangers
in this unrecognisable land.
Master,
this light burns through me;
this swelling music from the fringes of the soul
always growing closer.
I am burned by the lies Hope told me.
This body, burning,
these mirrors reflecting absolutely nothing.
Even the darkness burns.
There is nothing there,
not a thing.
Get yourself away from here.
Don't ever come back.
Perhaps this is a poem that never ends.

Conclusion

He had seen
nothing;
all around him
the ending of things, nothing more:
no towers
no stairways,
there wasn't even a song
to sing in all that desolation.

He was soaring high; so very high
he was pulled close

to his uttermost dreams
and suddenly tumbled back down,
plummeted
towards
the poem.

John Glenday

زستان له جیهاندا

ویلیام لیتفۆرد

پیرەژنەکە قاچەکانی بە کێش دەکرد بەناو بەفرەکەداو

ورد ورد شوێن پێیەکانی جێدەهما

تورەکەی بازاری کردنی پێ نیه

پێدەچێ لە کڵێسا بێتەوه

یان نا

دەشێ هەر پیاسەیەک بێت و ...

شەوەکانیش دورو درێژ

ئەو هێشتا توانای ماوەو ...

هەرەس نەگەیشتوه بەجەستەی

ئەو هێشتا لە ئێسکەکانی بەهێزتره

ئاوێزان نوری حکیم

85

شتاء العالم

ويليام لتفورد

بخطوات حذرة تكافح العجوز تاركة خطواتها في الثلج
لا أكياس تسوق، فربما هذه كنيسة، أو ربما ليست كذلك. ولأنها قادرة عليه؛ لعلها خرجت للمشي
حرةٌ هي الليلة
ولم تتضاءل
بل تبدو أكثر صلابة من العظم.

غريب اسكندر

Winter in the World

William Letford

The old lady struggles, footsteps careful, leaving shuffle marks in the snow
No shopping bag, so maybe it's church, and maybe not. Perhaps she is out
for a walk, because she can, and the night is spare, and she is undiminished
and harder than bone.

وەرزی بیرچوونەوە

ئاوێزان نوری حکیم

"با"بە تەنیشت ماڵمدا تێدەپەڕێ و...
بیری دەچێت دەرگاو پەنجەرەکەم بخاتە سەرپشت
پێڵاوەکانم دەرۆن و...
بیریان دەچێت پێیەکانم لەگەڵ خۆیاندا ببەن
"خەو"بەبەر چاومەوە سەما دەکات و...
بیری دەچێت بێتەسەر پێڵووەکانم
"خۆر"بە ئاسمانەوە هەڵدێ و...
بیری دەچێت سڵاو لە تاریکی ژوورەکەم بکات
"باران" بەخوڕ دادەکات و...
بیری دەچێت چۆڕێک ئاو بڕژێنێتە گەروی تینوێتییەوە
"یار"دەڕوات و بیری دەچێت بێتەوە
منیش لەتێ سێوی مردن دەخۆم و...
بیرم دەچێت هەندێکیش بۆنی ژیانەوە بکەم
لە وەرزی بیرچوونەوەدا
مندالەکانیش بیریان دەچێت پێ بگرن
عەیامێکە ژیان بایی کەس نابێ
جگە لە بیرچوونەوە
ئیمارەتێکم لە "فکر"دروستکردو...
ئیمبراتۆریەتی جەهل بردیە ڕێوە
خاکێکم بە عیشق تۆو کردو...
داری خیانەتی تیا ڕووا
مەعبەدێکم لەوەفا پڕکردو...
فەتوای نەمانی تیا درا
دەیان دەستنوێژی یەقینم هەڵگرت
جگە لە دووركات ترسو گومان
نوێژی جورئەتم پێ نەکرا

Oblivion Season

Awezan Nouri Hakeem

A wolf of wind, which passes my house
but forgets to huffpuff down my door

or this neglectful rain, which rains and pours
but forgets to slake thirst

which steals my shoes but leaves
my feet behind

or this blithe sun
oblivious to me in my dark room

as the lover is, who leaves me
and forgets to return

and the headlines on the newsprint of the clouds proclaim
'THIS IS OBLIVION SEASON'

The land I sowed with love
reverts to a wildwood of betrayal.

The temple I fed with my devotion
issues its fatwa of starvation.

One mouthful of the poisoned apple
and the spoor of life is lost again.

تا لەسەر وبەرمالّی وجود

وێردەکانم

ئاراستەی زانین بکەم و...

لە گوناهی نەزانین پاک ببمەوە

لە دامێنی خەیاڵێکی نارنجیشدا

دێری قەسیدەکانم

ئولفەتیان بە وشە ژەنگرتووەکانەوە گرت و...

خۆیان دووبارە کردەوە

ئیدی نازانم چی بنووسم

کە تەنها بیرچوونەوە میوانمه

نازانم من بیرم دەچێت برۆمە لای شیعر

یان شیعر بیری دەچێت ببێته میوانی پێنووسەکەم...

لەساڵی نەهامەتیدا

لەسەر پەڕاوی یادەوەری هەووردا

بە هێڵێکی گەورە نووسراوە

وەرزی بیرچوونەوە!!

My Emirate of Thought
consumed by the Empire of Ignorance.

Toddlers forget
to take their first steps.

Jen Hadfield

تصور أنك تسوق

جون غلانداي

تصور نفسك تسوق
الى لا مكان، مع (لا أحد) يجلس جانبك؛
في درب خالية مدورة، تنحلّ و تتكور
بتعاطف، مثلما مقود السيارة في يديك

على كلا الجانبين، حقل قمح يغادرك متلألئا
ماض في أصوات عصافير غائبة، و السماء
تصب ظلال الطقس في نفسها.
إذا إنك تواصل السياقة، آملا بالزمن وحده

عاليا، عندما ينتفض المحيط قبل أن تتشابه مع الغسق
و أنت أخيراً سوف تصنع اليابسة لتصل
ثمة قوارب طويلة النسيان و مهملة
و عندها كلاكما، حتما، ستلاحظان؛

مع ذلك أنا أخبرتكَ سابقاً، أن (لا أحد) يجلس جانبك
و ليس لكليكما اللامكان ليمضي.

صابرين كاظم

Imagine You are Driving

John Glenday

Imagine you are driving
nowhere, with no one beside you;
with the empty road unravelling and ravelling
in sympathy as the wheel turns in your hands.

On either side the wheatfields go shimmering
past in an absence of birdsong, and the sky
decants the shadows of the weather from itself.
So you drive on, hopeful of a time

when the ocean will rise up before you like dusk
and you will make landfall at last -
some ancient, long-forgotten mooring,
which both of you, of course, will recognise;

though as I said before, there is no one beside you
and neither of you has anywhere to go.

حق العودة أو ديمقراطية الوجود

زاهر موسى

ما رأيكم
أنْ نكسّرَ أنفسنا في المرايا؟
و نقشّرَ أجسادنا كالموز؟
و نطفئَ الضوءَ الذي يصيبنا بالنظر؟
و نخرجَ من الغرفة؟

ما رأيكم
أنْ نتركَ لزوجاتنا طلباتِ استقالة؟
و لأطفالنا تماثيلَ أباءٍ تُصنعُ من الحلوى؟
و لعائلاتنا نسخةً من (المسخ) لـ(كافكا)؟
و نخرجَ من البيت؟

ما رأيكم
أنْ نمحو وجوهَ الأزقة بأكتافنا المتدافعة؟
و نكشطَ الإسفلت إخفاءً لخطواتنا؟
و نكّني أسماء الشوارع و النصبِ و المحلات؟
و نخرجَ من المدينة؟

ما رأيكم
أنْ نبعثرَ اللغةَ بالهذيان؟
و نفرّقَ بين القلم و الورقة كروميو و جولييت؟
و نباعدَ بين القارات حتى تسقط الطائرات في الماء
و يموت البحارون جوعا؟
و نخرجَ من العالم؟

ما رأيكم
أنْ نثقبَ سورَ الجنةِ ببكارةِ أحلامنا؟

Right of Retreat
or Everyman's Guide to Beginning Again
Zaher Mousa

How about it?
We shatter ourselves against the mirror?
Peel back our skin like banana-skins?
Snuff out the light which forces us to witness?
And forget each room as we abandon it?

How about it?
We hand in letters of resignation to our wives?
And bags of jelly-baby Daddies-and-Mummies for the kids?
And for our folks, a copy of Kafka's 'Die Verwandlung'?
And then abandon the house?

How about it?
We use our scuffing shoulders to rub out those faces chalked on the alley
    walls?
Wear down flagstones to cover our own tracks?
Give stupid nicknames to the avenues, the statues, the High Street stores?
And finally abandon the city?

How about it?
We conflate Standard English and jibberish?
Lift pen from beloved paper - Juliet lost to her Romeo?
Drag continent further from continent, so baffled planes touch down on
    the sea
and sailors, ever sailing, die of hunger?
And abandon the world?

و نقفزَ فوق انهار الخمر كي لا نزدادَ سكراً؟

و نهمسَ للحور العين عن عجزنا الروحي؟

و نعودَ إلى آدم؟

How about it?

Shall we wither the battlements of Heaven with innocent dreams?

Vault rivers of promised wine to keep our heads clear?

Whisper to those doe-eyed houris: – "this impotence – it's not physical, you
  understand..."?

And finally; finally step backwards into Adam's footprints; Adam's bones?

John Glenday

It's Bleeding the Minutes Away

ساعتي التي تنزف الوقت

From 'The Doldrums'
(Zaher Mousa/ John Glenday)
Kufic Calligraphy by Samir Sumaida'ie

الطحالب

جين هادفيلد

أتساءلُ من سينصتُ كالطحالبِ
الملونةِ بالصمت؟!
أتساءلُ،
الملايينُ منهنَّ في دأبٍ بأذنٍ سوداء
و أخرى ذهبية،
من سينصتُ كذلك؟!
يا من تحفظ ما تسمعهُ مني
حديثي مع الطحالب فقط
تلك التي أتنفس في رئاتها
تتفحم مسامعها من جمرة صوتي
و ذهب الأفواه الصغيرة
تتسع خواتمه.

زاهر موسى

Lichen

Jen Hadfield

Who listens
like lichen listens

assiduous millions of black
and golden ears?

You hear and remember.
But I'm speaking

to the lichen.

The little ears prunk,
scorch and blacken.

The little golden mouths
gape.

عن ويتمان

غريب اسكندر

أغني نفسي
في أغنيتكَ الأخيرة
أغني نفسَكَ
في أغنيتي الأخيرة
كيف سنكتبهما إذن
العشب الذي اقترحته نسياناً
يتذكر الآن
الفرح الذي يسبق الكلمة
جذل أنا بها
مثلك
هذه الروح
الكلمة
التي تنمو كالعشب
ليست عشبة كلكامش
وليست عشبة المنفى
هذه التي تراها أمامَك
تنمو وحيدة
إنها عشبة الحقيقة
عشبة نوح التي سرقها العدم
عشبة أن يكون الشعر
ولا شيء غيره
الكلمة المتقدة بالعذاب
كان يكتب عن الألم
وحيداً
منفرداً به
بعذابات الليلة التي تمضي

On Whitman

Ghareeb Iskander

I sing myself
in your final song

I sing you
in my final song

  -- how can both
be written then?

The grass you suppose to be oblivion
remembers now
the delight the forerunner of the word –

I'm full of it
this soul.
The word which grows like grass
is not the elixir grass of Gilgamesh
nor the grass of exile
which you watch growing alone.

This is the grass of truth
Noah's grass snatched by nothingness
grass that becomes poetry
and nothing else –
the word blazing with pain.

سريعاً كلما

كان يكتب عن العزلة وإشراقها

عن معناها الأخير

عن ليله

ليل الألم

هذا الذي ينمو

كالعشب

أيضاً

يتمدد كالروح

على براري الجسد

كنهاراتنا المظلمة

دائماً وأبداً

لن أتحدث عنه تماماً

هذا الشاعر

يقيمه الأزل

ويكتبه النسيان

لن أتحدث عن ايمانه القديم

بالشعر

عن الملاك الذي فيه

عن نعت الكلمة بالمَجَرة

لن أتحدث عن لحيته الكثة

سأتحدث فقط

عن الصليب الذي فيه

أعمدة الموت

نص واحد وطويل

هو العمر

لذلك

أغني نفسي.

Exiled with pain,
he wrote about pain,
strained on the night's rack,
but when he wrote about aloneness, its radiance,
about his night of pain –
which grows grassly
and spreads like the soul
on the body's wild grassland plain –
which extends like our dark days
forever and never

it flew by.

I do not speak about the poet
immortalised by eternity
his poems ghostwritten by oblivion.

I do not speak of his abiding faith
in poetry the genie inside him
every word a galaxy

I will not speak of his grass-thick beard.

I speak only
of the cross inside him
pillars of death.

One long poem
like a long life.

This is why
I sing myself.

Jen Hadfield

بخصوص ذرات الروح

جون غلانداي

مرةً شرح لي شخص ما كيف أن القطع التي نتكون منها
تسقطُ بالسرعة نفسها
كما الكون.
ذراتنا، تسقط نحو مركز

أيما كلَّ شيء. ولا نراها.
نشعرُ فقط باحتكاكها الخفيف في ارتفاع اليد.
هذا هو الوزن،
هذه هي عملية السقوط الجماعي.
فضلاً عن ذلك، أن تلك الذرات تحمل كُلّابات

تمسك كُلّابات مثلها، كلُّ يقبض على نفسه
هذا ما يمنعنا من أن نكون شيئاً آخر،
ويفسر أننا في أيام الحب الأولى،
نشعرُ أحياناً بحبل القلب ممسكاً بقلب شخص آخر.

فقط ذرات الروح كرات تامة
ومن دون وسيلة للقبض على العالم
أو ربما لا حاجة لذلك،
فتتساقط عبر حياتنا التي لا تمسك سوى العدم، مثل مطر بهي،
وفي النهاية، كتَب، مازجةً في بئر الضوء الجماعي
في مركز ما نفترضه المركز، أو لعله ما كان مركزاً.

غريب اسكندر

Concerning the Atoms of the Soul

John Glenday

Someone explained once how the pieces of what we are
fall downwards at the same rate
as the Universe.
The atoms of us, falling towards the centre

of whatever everything is. And we don't see it.
We only sense their slight drag in the lifting hand.
That's what weight is, that communal process of falling.
Furthermore, these atoms carry hooks, like burrs,

hooks catching like hooks, like clinging to like,
that's what keeps us from becoming something else,
and why in early love, we sometimes
feel the tug of the heart snagging against another's heart.

Only the atoms of the soul are perfect spheres
with no means of holding on to the world
or perhaps no need for holding on,
and so they fall through our lives catching

against nothing, like perfect rain,
and in the end, he wrote, mix in that common well of light
at the centre of whatever the suspected
centre is, or might have been.

ثلاث قصائد

غريب اسكندر

I

دعيني أكتب عنكِ
قصيدة غزل
سأقول فيها عنكِ:
ليست طويلة تماماً
وليست لها عينان زرقاوان
وشعرها لم يكن بلون الذهب
ويداها
لا أعرف كيف أصفهما
قلبها فقط
مَن أتاح لي
أن أسمو على مدارج النهاية.

II

كلاهما يُدمي القلب
الرحيل إليه
أو الرحيل منه
الوطن أو المنفى
خروجكِ، تلك الليلة،
أو بقاؤكِ
عيناكِ اللتان يتلألأ فيهما الدمع
أو المطر الذي تتلألأ خلاله النافذة
غيابكِ وحضوركِ
ليس ثمة فرق
في هذه الصحراء
الشاسعة كالروح!

Three Poems

Ghareeb Iskander

I

I want you to let me write you a ghazal
that says:
She's not particularly tall,
her eyes hold not a spark of blue,
her hair is nothing like the colour of gold
and her hands - well I don't quite know
how to describe those hands...
only her heart, that true compass,
guides me without knowing
where I need to go.

II

Home or exile,
to abandon; to remain,
both bleed in the same heart.
Either your eyes, bright with crying
or rain caught in sunlight, falling beyond the window.
Your presence or your absence -
it really doesn't matter which
in that small country
where there are no tears and there is no rain.

III

المقهى هو هو

الموسيقى هي هي

النافذة

الطاولات

عاملة المقهى

منفضة السجائر الوحيدة في الخارج

كل شيْ مثل كل شيء

مع ذلك

لم تكن هي

كان ثمة شيء منها

يطوف في المكان

الذي كان هو هو

في زمان لم يكن

هو هو

- ما هذا؟

- لا أعرف!

III

the old cafe hadn't changed at all:
same music,
same window,
same tables,
same waitress,
even that same ashtray set outside the door.
Everything still looked exactly like everything.

But she was no longer she

and something of her haunted that restless place,
that identical place, locked in a different time.
And what or when or where it was - who knows?

John Glenday

پیاوی داقنشی
جۆن گلاندی

جارێکیان هەولمدا خەیاڵ
چێوەی بازنەی ڕوح بکەم
بەلام ئەوەی پێی گەیشتم
تروسکایی هەتاوێکی شیری شین
بڵقی فکرێکی باڵ
بە باڵام هێمای سفر.
هەموو ئەمانە لە پڕ بیری خستمەوە
بەو بازنەیەی جارێکیان
بە ڕاماڵینی دەستە بەحیرەکانی کێشای
گەیاندیە دەرەوەی تۆڕی جەستەی خۆی و ...
پڕیی کرد بە هیچدا

ئاوێزان نوری حکیم

114

Vitruvian Man

John Glenday

There was a time I tried picturing
the circumference of the soul
but the best I could manage

was a shimmery, milk-blue sun,
an oversized thought-bubble,
a zero with my height

which immediately reminded me
of that hoop he once transcribed
through a sweep of his sepia arms,

as he reached out beyond
the trammel of himself and caught hold
of nothing with both hands.

ملل

زاهر موسى

جرحٌ في اليد
تلك هي ساعتي التي تنزفُ الوقتَ
وتبددهُ دونَ قيمة

أيها النهار
لقد جئتَ وذهبتَ كامرأةٍ في حافلة

أبداً ، لا يشبه النهرَ المنسابَ دمي
يشفُّ ويزدادُ بطئاً عاماً بعد عام
أفكرُ بساعتي التي دارت كثيرا على نفسها
وبثوانيها التي تنفرط.

The Doldrums

Zaher Mousa

I

I'll carry this wound like a wristwatch - look,
it's bleeding the minutes away;
but leaves no mark, no scar on Time
though day wears day down into day.

II

Dear afternoon, I only glimpsed you as you sailed past
my window and vanished forever,
like that girl on the bus,
that utterly, hopelessly, beautiful girl.

III

No. My blood is nothing like the honest river
glazing and slackening, season through season.
Think of a worn-out wall-clock with its dodgy weathers:
faster and faster, then slower again, then…

John Glenday

نا تاریک

جۆن گلاندی

کەنیشکەکان وا دەگەڕێنەوە ئەوانەی

وێنەی میلی کاتژمێرەکانیان بە روناکی کێشاو مردن

دەگەڕێنەوەو دەستەکانیان دەدرەوشێتەوە

لە کاتێکدا لێوەکانیان، پرچەکانیان، هەنگاوی پێیەکانیان

لە دوێنێدا چەشنی کلوە بەفرێکی نامۆ دەدرەوشێتەوە

وەکو ئەوەی رۆژانێک، ئەو تیشکەی لەواندا پرشنگی دەدا

هەڵهاتبێ و

گڕی لە پەموی ژینیان دا

من دەمەوێ بزانم، ئەوان چۆن باوەڕیان هێنا

شتێک بەو هەموو جوانیەوە دەبێتە کامەرانیان

سەرەرای ئەوەی چۆن لێوەکانیان دەپشکوێ بۆ وەڵامدانەوەم

جگە لە درەوشانە هیچ نابیستم

ئاوێزان نوری حکیم

Undark

John Glenday

And so they come back, those girls who painted
the watch dials luminous, and died.

The come back and their hands glow and their lips
and hair and their footprints gleam in the past like alien snow.

It was as if what shone in them once had broken free
and burned through the cotton of their lives.

And I want to know this: I want to know how they came to believe
that something so beautiful could ever have turned out right,

but though they open their mouths to answer me,
all I can hear is light.

Credits

Translations

All bridge translations from Arabic into English, and vice versa, were provided by Lauren Pyott. All bridge translations from Kurdish into English, and vice versa, were provided by Hoshang Waziri.

Acknowledgements

This book and the Reel Iraq translation project would not have been possible without the support of the British Council and British Council Iraq, Literature Across Frontiers, Creative Scotland, Stars Hotel, Scottish Poetry Library, Bakehouse, Rich Mix, Henry Bell and the Poetry Club, the Arab British Centre, Cultures of Resistance, British Institute for the Study of Iraq, the Iraqi Student Project, the International Arab Charity, the Forest, and many more friends and organisations to which we are extremely grateful. Thank you to the Reel Festivals team and volunteers, and of course many thanks to the staff at Freight Books for making this publication happen. Reel Iraq 2013 was a Firefly International Project.

About Reel Festivals

Reel Festivals organises festivals, events and workshops to explore alternative stories through direct interaction and shared experiences. By collaborating with artists working across, film, literature, music and theatre, we aim to build solidarity with communities and individuals in times of conflict. Previous projects have focused on Syria, Lebanon, Iraq and Afghanistan, with a central focus on poetry, music and film. For more information, news and videos from projects go to: www.reelfestivals.org